INTRODUCTION

East of the Cascade Mountains lies a vast land made aromatic by the scent of Sagebrush. Long tongues of this sagebrush country extend northward into some British Columbia valleys. Eastward, it reaches in places to the Rocky Mountains, and southward it eventually merges into the Mojave Desert, far south of the area covered by this book. We are concerned here with the dry, open land from the Thompson River Valley in B.C. southward to Highway 26 in Oregon, and from the Cascade Mountains eastward to Spokane and the Snake River.

This book illustrates most of the showiest of the spring wildflowers of this area. It is intended to be carried with you in the field to help you identify these plants, at least in their broader groups.

Several major highlands or mountain ranges are within this big sagebrush country. The Blue Mountains and the Wallowas of Oregon are examples, and much of northeast Washington is highland. These places are heavily forested, or rise above the timberline. Their forest flowers will be included in a later book. Sagebrush, however, grows mainly on lower slopes.

Some botanists would describe this book's area as the northern extension of the Great Basin. I prefer to name it after its dominant plant — "sagebrush country." Perhaps a birdwatcher might call it "magpie country."

This land is characterized by its dryness. Damp air moving eastward from the Pacific Ocean rises and cools when it reaches the Cascade Mountains and the Coast Range in B.C. and falls as rain. Thus, the western slopes of these mountains are moist, and can support giant Douglas Fir forests. But on the eastern side, the average annual precipitation is only 10 to 16 inches (25 cm. to 40 cm.) a year. This is semi-desert, baking-hot and dry in summer, and cold and dry in winter.

To survive here, plants must be adapted to the harsh environment. You can see for yourself that most have small leaves. These are adequate to catch the abundant sunshine, but small enough to minimize loss of water to the wind. Notice, too, that many are covered with silvery hairs. These slow the wind on the leaf surface, helping to reduce moisture loss. Some have special parts in which to store water, while others extend their roots remarkably deep into the ground to find moisture.

A further adaptation common to most of these plants is that they rush into bloom in the spring, and so avoid the problem of having to sustain growth during summer's drought. Therefore, the best time to see them is usually some time in late May.

As you travel the sagebrush country you will soon find that there are several easily discernible variations in habitat-type, and that the various plants tend to show a preference for one particular habitat. Sagebrush prefers the really arid ground. Sometimes this means the rolling plains of open "scabland", and sometimes the lower slopes of the valleys. A fair amount of such land is under cultivation. Where that is the case watch for rocky outcrops where the soil is too thin for the farmer. Here the Sagebrush and wildflowers will likely still thrive. These are places for *Phlox, Eriogonum, Allium* and *Penstemon*. Very different are the seasonal watercourses and damp "seeps" where soil water lasts longer. Here you may watch for such treasures as *Hesperochiron*, and, perhaps, a spectacular clump of *Iris missouriensis*.

Still another variation occurs where the Sagebrush meets the scattered pines of the forests above. Watch here for *Sisyrinchium douglasii*, or *Mertensia longiflora*. Gullies and canyon bottoms are favored by the larger shrubs, and *Balsamorhiza* usually does best on deep-soiled sunny slopes.

A few kinds of wildflowers are particularly common in sagebrush country. Each kind occurs as a complex of species. There are, for example, many kinds of *Eriogonums, Erigerons, Penstemons, Lupines* and *Phlox*. In some instances it takes an expert to sort these into their exact species. We think, however, that most readers

3

will be content to identify an *Eriogonom* or a *Phlox* as such when they find one, without attempting the more difficult task of deciding its precise species. Therefore we are giving each of these important groups a full page, but illustrating it with just three or four representative species.

English or "common" plant names are a problem. None of them are "official", in that no comprehensive list has gained universal acceptance. Indeed many wildflowers have acquired several local names in different parts of their ranges. Obviously it is important that we not make the situation worse by inventing more! In selecting common names we have given preference to those in the late Lewis J. Clark's scholarly works. His choices were wise, and he is widely read. For species he does not list we have gone next to "*A Field Guide to Pacific States Wildflowers*" by Niehaus and Ripper. However, it deals largely with areas south of ours, so we are still left with a few plants lacking common names. In such cases we have simply used the first part of the standard binomial Latin name. Nothing could be safer!

Books for serious botanists list plants by plant families in an accepted order, and this works well for botanists. This, however, often widely separates unrelated kinds that happen to look alike, so it doesn't work well for the amateur. Here the plants are grouped primarily by flower color, with the large shrubs placed at the start of each color section. In the case of the most common plant groups, the various color forms are brought together in the color group most typical of the plant. Purple and blue are the most difficult to categorize because in nature they often occur together on a single flower, or as variations in one kind of flower.

Don't drive into sagebrush country expecting to see miles and miles of wildflowers. There are places where they make a brave show, but there are extensive areas where there is little more than Sagebrush. Also there are hundreds of thousands of acres in which wildflowers have been eradicated by agriculture. The wildflowers that remain are a heritage that we should all help to protect. Above all, don't pick them or dig them for your garden. They are not suited to normal garden soils and culture, and will almost surely die. Leave them for everyone to enjoy!

Sagebrush Wildflowers

J.E. (Ted) Underhill

hancock
house

ISBN 0-88839-171-4

Copyright © 1986 J.E. Underhill

Canadian Cataloging in Publication Data

Underhill, J.E., 1919 —
  Sagebrush wildflowers

(Wildflower series)
Includes index.
ISBN 0-88839-171-4

1. Wild flowers — Northwest, Pacific —
Identification. I. Title. II. Series
QK203.B7U49   582.13'09711   C83-091107-3

Edited by Diana Ottosen
Typeset by Elizabeth Grant
Layout/production by Dorothy Forbes

Front cover photos: Sumach and rabbitbrush
                    Gilia aggregata
Back cover photo: Erigeron linearis

Printed in Hong Kong

Published simultaneously in Canada and the United States by

HANCOCK HOUSE PUBLISHERS LTD.
19313 Zero Ave., Surrey, B.C. V3S 5J9
HANCOCK HOUSE PUBLISHERS INC.
1431 Harrison Avenue, Blaine, WA 98230

MOCK ORANGE
Philadelphus lewisii Lustingl

Also found in upland areas

- shrub averaging 5 to 7 ft. (1.5 m. to 2 m.)
- mainly in gullies and by seasonal watercourses
- leaves are deeply veined with small, regular teeth

The best forms of this choice shrub are sold in nurseries. Many are sweet-scented. Don't cut or dig the wild plants!

5

SASKATOON BERRY
Amelanchier alnifolia

Muchownik

Also found in coastal and upland areas

- shrub usually 5 to 10 ft. (1.5 m. to 3 m.)
- mainly in gullies, canyon bottoms and seeps
- leaves with forward-pointing teeth on outer third

The dark purple berries were mixed with meat to make the "pemmican" of the Indians.

SQUAW CURRANT

Ribes cereum

Also found in upland areas

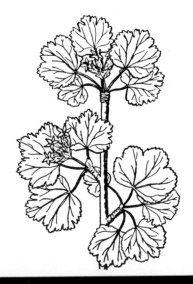

- shrub from 3 to 5 ft (1 m. to 1.5 m.)
- on dry slopes or by watercourses
- leaves lobed, toothed, hairy

The flowers vary from white to a pale pink. The rather spectacular scarlet berries look delicious, but have a very poor flavor.

SANDWORT

Arenaria franklinii *Pčeunice*

- low, tufted herb to about 4 inches (10 cm.)
- with Sagebrush on arid ground
- leaves very small, sharply tapering

Sandwort somewhat resembles a small *Phlox*, but does not have the flower extending as a long tube beneath as in *Phlox*. There are several kinds in sagebrush country.

BASTARD TOAD-FLAX
Comandra umbellata

Also found in upland areas

- herb about 8 to 10 inches (20 cm. to 25 cm.)
- with grass and Sagebrush
- leaves fairly narrow, equally spaced, alternate up the stem

This Comandra is a widespread though inconspicuous plant. At maturity it has small purple berries. It also grows far beyond the range of Sagebrush.

WHITE VIRGIN'S BOWER
Clematis ligusticifolia

- vine growing along fences or over shrubs
- common in the valleys
- leaves compound, coarsely toothed

This small-flowered *Clematis* is abundant and easily seen in the northwestern valleys of our area.

OENOTHERA
Oenothera pallida *Enjulka*

- short herb to about 12 inches (30 cm.)
- favors sandy banks in full sun
- note pink buds atop long pink ovaries

Even Sagebrush scarcely ventures onto the parched sands where this *Oeno-thera* thrives. There are related species in yellow, often taller, and demanding much moister ground.

SAND LILY
Leucocrinum montanum

- short herb to about 6 inches (15 cm.)
- usually with Sagebrush on dry outcrops
- leaves long, "strap-like"; flowers have six petals

The spectacular and sweet-scented Sand Lily grows in parts of Oregon and southward.This lily is a treasure that should on no account be picked or collected.

HESPEROCHIRON

Hesperochiron pumilis

- dwarf herbs to about 2 inches (5 cm.)
- usually in grass on moist seeps
- few leaves almost flat on the ground

Two quite similar species of *Hesperochiron* occur within our area. Watch for them where moisture seeps to the soil's surface in late May.

YARROW (Milfoil)
Achillea millefolium

Also found in upland areas

- herb to about 25 in. (60 cm.)
- widespread from coast to subalpine
- foliage finely divided, hairy, strongly aromatic

Yarrow is widely distributed in the northern hemisphere. Like many other strong-smelling herbs it has been used for medicinal purposes since ancient times.

HOARY CRESS
Cardaria draba

- herb from 8 to 10 in. (20 to 25 cm.)
- in conspicuous colonies in pastures and waste places
- leaf bases point back around the stem; leaves hairy

Hoary Cress spreads by underground runners to make large patches that are quite striking when in flower. It belongs to the Mustard family.

SILVER LEAF PHACELIA

Phacelia hastata   *Ivasenka*

- herb to about 18 inches (50 cm.)
- occurs on dry, sandy places—roadsides are a favorite
- leaves silver-haired

The flower color varies to mauve. Note
the prominent anthers, and the way the
flowers grow in coiled clusters.

POISON IVY
Rhus radicans

- shrub from 1 to 3 feet (30 cm. to 1 m.)
- widespread in gullies and on roadsides
- drooping leaflets in threes, often with a few coarse teeth

Learn to know and avoid Poison Ivy, because contact with it causes severe dermatitis in many people. The leaves turn a handsome red in autumn.

FRINGE CUP
Lithophragma glabra

- herb usually about 10 to 12 inches (25 to 30 cm.)
- widespread companion of Sagebrush
- leaves deeply cut; 3 to 5 cleft petals

At least two fairly similar species of Fringe Cup are in the area. Both have the distinctive cleft flowers.

PUSSY-TOES
Antennaria stenophylla

- herb to about 10 inches (25 cm.)
- scattered with the Sagebrush on dry sites
- leaves silky-haired

About half-a-dozen kinds of these rather dingy little daisies occur in our area. In a few instances the flowers may have a pink tinge.

COMMON SAGEBRUSH
Artemisia tridentata

- straggling, branched shrub 2 to 5 feet (.6 to 1.5 m.)
- characteristic of whole area
- main leaves wedge-shaped; three teeth at the tips

Sagebrush gets its common name from the supposed resemblance of its aromatic smell to that of the kitchen sage, which is a *Salvia* and not related. Note that Sagebrush has silver-haired foliage.

ANTELOPE BUSH
(Greasewood)

Purshia tridentata

- shrub about 5 to 7 feet (1.5 to 2.5 m.)
- widespread with Sagebrush in B.C., Washington and Oregon
- leaves three-toothed, dark green

Don't confuse Antelope Bush with Sagebrush, which is smaller and has pale gray-haired leaves. In both the leaves are three-toothed.

RABBIT BRUSH
Chrysothamnus nauseosus

- twiggy shrub, usually 3 to 5 feet (1 to 1.5 m.)
- widespread with Sagebrush
- leaves very narrow, long, silver-haired

Rabbit Brush is another shrub which some people confuse with Sagebrush, although the long, toothless leaves make it quite different. Its golden flowers are a feature of late summer.

W. MERILEES

BALSAM ROOT
(Spring Sunflower)

Balsamorhiza sagittata

- herbs usually about 2 to 2½ feet (.6 to .8 m.)
- open hillsides in sagebrush country
- leaves large, basal, with broad, hairy blades

Several fairly similar species of Balsam Root make bold splashes of gold on the hillsides in early spring. The roots and seeds were important foods for Indians of the area.

MULES' EARS
Wyethia amplexicaulis

- robust herbs to about 2 feet (.6 m.)
- favors slopes that hold moisture
- leaves hairless, shiny, clasp the stalk

Mules' Ears are superficially similar to Balsam Root, but the shiny bright green leaves provide an obvious distinction.

SUNFLOWER

Helianthus cusickii /hmecmic

- herb to about 3 feet (1 m.)
- sporadic with the Sagebrush
- lower leaves lance-shaped, opposite

These large-flowered daisies often occur with or near Balsam Root, but are easily distinguished by their smaller leaves, and because their leaves are well up on the stem.

BROWN-EYED SUSAN

Gaillardia aristata *Kohardy*

- herb to about 16 to 24 inches (40 to 60 cm.)
- B.C. and Washington within our area
- leaves rough-haired, with few coarse teeth or lobes

Gaillardia is most common in the north of the sagebrush country, often in showy colonies. Each petal is tipped with three lobes.

OYSTER PLANT
Tragopogon dubius

Also found in coastal and upland areas

- herb from about 2 to 3½ feet (.7 to 1 m.)
- common along roadsides
- leaves long, grassy, inconspicuous

The flowers are followed by big, dandelion-like seed heads atop the slender blue-green foliage. The species was introduced here from Europe. The flowers open only in sunshine.

HAWKSBEARD
Crepis modocencis

- herb to about 12 inches (30 cm.)
- with Sagebrush and Phlox on dry ground
- leaves mainly basal, deeply toothed

This, to our thinking, is the handsomest of the Hawksbeards, which are generally a scrawny lot. It is not common in our experience.

TOWER BUTTERWEED
Senecio integerrimus *bur ĕ ĕ w*

- herb to about 3 feet (1 m.)
- favors ditchbanks, old pastures and moist seeps
- leaves spoon-shaped below, lance-shaped above

This Butterweed is widespread and common in our area.

OREGON SUNSHINE

Eriophyllum lanatum

Also found in coastal and upland areas

- herb usually about 12 inches (30 cm.) but variable
- rock crevices and stony ground
- leaves and stems woolly — leaf shapes various

A typical habitat for the Oregon Sunshine is a roadside cliff. In some forms the leaves are toothed, in others they are not.

FLEABANE
Erigeron linearis   Turan

- herb to about 12 inches (30 cm.) tall
  — often less
- dry, stony locations, often with Sagebrush
- leaves long, very narrow

There are several other fairly similar yellow-flowered Fleabane species in sagebrush country. See also the mauve and pink Fleabanes on page 54.

PRICKLY PEAR CACTUS

Opuntia fragilis

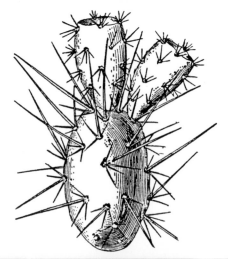

- short, mat-forming herb to about 3 inches (7 cm.)
- widespread on sandy ground, often with Sagebrush
- stems are **swollen rounded pads** bearing **clusters of spines**

Step cautiously when in cactus country, for the sharp spines can pierce light shoes and inflict a painful wound.

TANSYLEAF SUN CUP
Oenothera tanacetifolia

- short, tufted herb to about 3 inches (7 cm.)
- damp seeps from Washington southward
- leaves basal, much crimped, deeply toothed

This is one of the nicest of the Sun Cups, a group closely related to the Evening Primrose of our gardens.

BLAZING STAR
Mentzelia laevicaulis

- open, branched herb usually 12 to 16 inches (30 to 40 cm.)
- prefers dry, open sites
- leaves deeply toothed; whole plant unpleasant to touch

Blazing Star is easy to miss because the big flowers open only in sunshine, and without them the plant is inconspicuous.

LEWIS'S LOMATIUM

Lomatium triternatum

- herb, usually 12 to 24 inches (30 to 60 cm.)
- common with Sagebrush
- leaves divided

The whole plant bears resemblance to Parsley or Carrot, to which it is related. Flower color is most often yellow, but white and purple kinds also occur.

Lomatium macrocarpum

WESTERN WALLFLOWER

Erysimum occidentale ~~Trynel~~

- herb, usually unbranched, from 12 to 20 inches (30 to 50 cm.)
- common with Sagebrush
- leaves narrow, gray-green

The long, narrow seed pods stand almost vertical after the flowers have gone.

CLEOMELLA
Cleomella macbrideana

- annual herb to about 16 inches (40 cm.)
- dry, sandy slopes in parts of central Oregon
- leaves of three leaflets

Cleomella usually occurs in large, spectacular colonies. To add to their attraction, the flowers are fragrant.

THE BUCKWHEATS
Eriogonum spp.

Buckwheats in variety and abundance decorate the sagebrush country. It is interesting that the Sagebrush is virtually the same everywhere, but that every few miles you'll find a fresh species or color form of Buckwheat. They vary in form from very compact (as *E. douglasii*) to quite robust (as *E. compositus*). In color they vary from white through cream to yellow and into bright rose, and the individual flowers commonly turn color as they mature. Species illustrated all have compact heads consisting of many flowers, but there are other kinds in which the flowers are held well apart.

Eriogonum douglasii (above)
Eriogonum thymoides (opposite)
Eriogonum compositus (below)

THOMPSON'S PAINTBRUSH
Castilleja thompsonii

- herb, usually 8 to 12 inches (20 to 30 cm.)
- common with Sagebrush, south B.C. and Washington
- leaves long, narrow below, 3 to 5 forked above

As the picture shows, this species often has stems and calyces tinged with purple. The actual flowers are tubular, and hard to see amongst the yellow bracts and leaves.

BEARDED OWL'S CLOVER
Orthocarpus barbatus

- hairy herb to about 8 inches (20 cm.)
- sagebrush country in central and east Washington
- bracts much broader than the lower leaves

All the leaves have long, slender lobes. The close relationship to *Castilleja* is evident.

PUCCOON (Western Gromwell)

Lithospermum ruderale *Kamejia*

- much branched herb, usually 16 to 20 inches (40 to 50 cm.)
- widespread in our area
- leaves long, narrow, rough-haired, not toothed

Puccoon's flowers are not large, but the plant has a way of standing out as a solid mass of green and yellow against a background that is usually grayer or browner.

THE LOCOWEEDS

Astragalus spp.
Oxytropis spp. ~~Kohinee~~

These are two closely allied groups in the Pea family, with differences that matter only to a botanist. They earn the name "Locoweed" because some kinds are toxic to livestock, and have become of considerable concern to ranchers. There are many species and they are common companions of Sagebrush. Color varies from white through yellow to pink and purple. Some of the most attractive have silvery foliage and flowers of a fair size, but many kinds are small-flowered and insignificant.

Astragalus inflexus

Oxytropis campestris

Astragalus convallarius

DEATH CAMAS
Zigadenus venenosus

- bulbous herb, usually 12 to 16 inches (30 to 40 cm.)
- widespread in our area
- leaves long, grassy, narrow

Two rather similar species accompany Sagebrush. Both are very poisonous, and sometimes killed Indians who mistook the bulbs for those of the edible Camas, hence the name.

BUTTER-AND-EGGS

Linaria vulgaris ~~Linaka~~

- erect herb, usually about 16 to 24 inches (40 to 60 cm.)
- introduced and spreading rapidly
- leaves blue-green, narrow, lacking teeth

This plant looks like a slender Snapdragon (and is related). It has been brought in from the Mediterranean region, and is spreading rapidly by both seeds and running roots. In places it is already a severe problem for farmers.

COMMON MULLEIN

Verbascum thapsus *Divina*

Also found in coastal and upland areas

- tall herb, usually 5 to 7 feet (1.5 to 2 m.)
- widespread on roadside and waste ground
- leaves mostly basal, large, woolly, yellowish

This is another plant that has been brought from Europe and thrives here. Because it is large and grows in colonies it attracts much attention. Again, it is a Snapdragon relative.

HOPSAGE

Grayia spinosa

- dense, gray shrub to about 4½ feet (1.5 m.)
- very dry areas, central Washington & Oregon
- leaves small, rough; twigs often spiny

The colored bractlets (modified upper leaves) vary from whitish to red. In its best color varieties it is a strikingly handsome shrub.

WHITE-LEAVED GLOBE MALLOW

Sphaeralcea munroana

- shrubby perennial to about 24 inches (60 cm.)
- roadsides and dry banks
- leaves shallowly lobed, with star-shaped hairs

A patch of this Globe Mallow makes a striking sight. The flower color varies to pink, and there are related species. The smaller species *S. coccinea* has compound leaves and similar scarlet flowers.

SUMAC
Rhus glabra *Shumpy*

- sparse shrub from 1 to 9 feet (30 cm. to 3 m.)
- widespread near watercourses, often forming large colonies
- leaves very large and compound — bright red in autumn

Sumac actually has inconspicuous yellow flowers that few people see. It is the bright red leaves that make it striking. The name is not Indian but Arabic in origin.

THE PHLOXES

Phlox spp. *Slqmenka*

A variety of *Phlox* species occur with Sagebrush. Most are bright pink, but a few are white or mauve. All are tufted herbs of about 4 to 12 inches (10 to 30 cm.) with narrow leaves that are usually short, but may be long. In all, and in some related plants, the flower disc extends beneath as a long tube. Usually, where you see Phlox, there are other kinds of wildflowers growing close by.

Phlox viscida (above)
Phlox longifolia (opposite)

Phlox longifolia in the Okanagan

43

THE WILD ONIONS
Allium spp.

There are over two dozen kinds of Wild Onions in the Pacific Northwest, roughly half of them being found with or close to the Sagebrush. Almost all have an unmistakable garlic aroma when their foliage is crushed. The leaves of some kinds are very slender and rounded, and are scarcely noticeable at flowering. In others the leaves are flattened and strap-like.

Allium geyeri (above)
Allium acuminatum (opposite)
Allium parvum (below)

SCARLET GILIA

Gilia aggregata

Also found in upland areas

- biennial herb to about 24 inches (60 cm.)
- wide-ranging on dry ground
- leaves much divided, hairy

Red flowers are usual, but the color varies to yellow, or even white. The plant dies after it has seeded.

LARGE-FLOWERED COLLOMIA
Collomia grandiflora

- annual herb, usually about 16 inches (40 cm.)
- widespread, but seldom abundant in our area
- leaves narrow, rough-haired

The flowers are often a unique salmon-pink color. Note that the two kinds of plants illustrated on these pages have their flowers extended as long tubes beneath. In this they are similar to *Phlox,* to which they are related.

W. MERILEES

MICROSTERIS
Microsteris gracilis

- small herb, averaging about 4 inches (10 cm.)
- widespread with Sagebrush and in other zones
- leaves without teeth, usually hairy

Observe the notched petals, and the yellow or white throat of the flower. These flowers are the tiniest in this book, being only ¼ inch (5 mm.) across.

HOARY CHAENACTIS
(Dusty Maiden)
Chaenactis douglasii

- sparsely branched herb to about 20 inches (50 cm.)
- far-ranging but seldom very abundant
- leaves doubly compound, gray-haired, "lacy"

Flower color in this *Chaenactis* species varies from pink to a dingy white, and the stem and leaves are usually flushed with color.

SPOTTED KNAPWEED
Centaurea maculosa

- sparsely branched herb of about 24 inches (60 cm.)
- introduced weed, spreading rapidly
- leaves compound, rough-haired

The flower color is usually pink or mauve, but varies to white. Biologists have brought in insects that eat Knapweed for it has become a serious agricultural problem. In late summer it snaps off at ground level and the wind rolls it across open land to scatter its seeds. It is thus one of several species of tumbleweed.

A. GRASS

SATIN FLOWER
Sisyrinchium douglasii

Also found in coastal areas

- slender herb from about 6 to 8 inches (15 to 20 cm.)
- seasonally moist ground in parts of the sagebrush country
- leaves slender, inconspicuous

Satin Flowers we have seen near Sagebrush have been a lovely clear pink, quite unlike the rich purple of the same species at the coast.

SHOWY MILKWEED
Asclepias speciosa

- robust herb to about 3 feet (1 m.)
- on ditchbanks and beside water-courses
- leaves broad, large; in opposite pairs

Milkweed earns its name from its copious, sticky latex. The large, inflated seed pods produce silky fibre that was used in wartime to fill lifejackets. Leaves of Milkweed are the sole food of caterpillars of the monarch butterfly.

Milkweed seed pods

BITTER ROOT (Spaetlum)

Lewisia rediviva

- short, tufted herb, scarcely 2 inches (5 cm.)
- often in large colonies on sandy ground
- often leafless when flowering; tufts of linear leaves in fall

Color in this species varies from near white to a rich rose pink. The blossoms open only in sunshine, and you may miss it entirely at other times.

PURPLE AVENS

Geum triflorum *Kuh li' k*

- herb to about 12 inches (30 cm.)
- common on moist seeps
- main leaves compound, with toothed leaflets

Triflorum means three-flowered, and indeed the flowers usually grow in threes. The stems and leaves are generally quite hairy.

THE PENSTEMONS

Penstemon spp.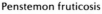

There may be as many as two dozen kinds of Penstemons within our area. Most are long-living perennials, woody at the base, deep-rooted, and given to living in rock crevices and on talus slopes. Some, however, choose the dry, arid flatter ground. Mauve and blue are the principal colors, but there are white and yellow kinds. The leaves are generally lance-like. In some kinds they are toothed. Look carefully and you will see their obvious kinship with the Snapdragon of our gardens.

Penstemon deustus

Penstemon fruticosis

THE FLEABANES

Erigeron spp.

Erigerons are common companions of Sagebrush, there being at least fifteen species within our area. Most are short, tufted little plants with a very attractive appearance. Pink and mauve are the usual colors, but there are almost as many to be seen in golden yellow (see page 28 for an example). The leaves vary but are never big and coarse. The mauve flowers may remind you of *Asters* but Asters bloom in late summer, while these *Erigerons* almost all bloom in spring.

Erigeron filifolius (above)
Erigeron compositus (opposite)
Erigeron divergens (below)

WESTERN BLUE FLAG

Iris missouriensis *Koratec*

- herb to about 24 inches (60 cm.)
- fairly common on damp seeps in sagebrush country
- leaves long, narrow, much flattened

This striking *Iris* spreads by underground rhizomes, and often forms very large colonies. The flower color varies from whitish to blue or purple.

MARIPOSA LILY

Calochortus macrocarpus

Pehnosemenee

- herb to about 18 inches (50 cm.)
- common with Sagebrush
- leaves few, narrow, inconspicuous

This lovely wildflower blooms in mid-summer. Unfortunately it is being quickly destroyed by grazing animals and by being picked, so it is becoming scarcer.

MAHALA MAT

Ceanothus prostratus

- small sub-shrub, flat on the ground
- S. central Washington through Oregon, in light timber
- leaves holly-like, but smaller and softer

Most people miss this beautiful little shrub nestled amidst the pine needles because its soft colors are hard to see from a distance.

DOUGLAS'S TRITELIA
Tritelia douglasii

- herb to about 18 inches (50 cm.)
- common on grassy ground in our area
- leaves narrow, long, inconspicuous

There are several rather similar species of *Tritelia*, and they are not always easy to sort out. This kind's strongly wavy petals are one of its distinguishing features.

SAGE
Salvia dorii *Salvej*

- broad shrub to about 24 inches (60 cm.)
- on dry banks with Sagebrush
- leaves silver-haired, not toothed

Dry, exposed banks are favored by this coarse, often spiny shrub. It belongs to the mint family, but somewhat resembles a *Penstemon* until examined closely.

THE LUPINES

Lupinus spp.

You literally cannot drive through this country without seeing Lupines in late spring. Most are robust plants from 2 to 2½ feet (.6 to .75 m.). The leaves are always compound, with a rounded outline, and the numerous leaflets meet at a point that is not quite central. Some kinds are silky-haired. Purple and blue are the most common colors, but some have white or yellow flowers. Single plants may display quite a bit of pink. Look closely, and you can see that the individual flowers clearly mark Lupines as members of the Pea family.

Lupinus laxiflorus

Lupinus argenteus

WILD DELPHINIUM
Delphinium spp.

- herbs, usually about 8 to 16 inches (20 to 40 cm.)
- common in sagebrush country
- leaves compound about a central point, much divided

Several rather similar kinds of *Delphinium* grow in the area. Most are slender plants with little branching. Some are notable for being toxic to livestock that eat them.

NARROW-LEAVED PHACELIA

Phacelia linearis

- annual herb, variably 4 to 18 inches (10 to 50 cm.)
- widespread in the dry country
- upper leaves often three-lobed

Here is a plant so variable in size that it often deceives the viewer who may not recognize it as the species seen just yesterday.

LUNGWORT
Mertensia longiflora

- herbs, usually about 4 inches (10 cm.)
- fairly frequent where Sagebrush meets the forest
- a few soft stem leaves on flowering plants

Lungwort often grows in spectacular, large colonies. Two fairly similar species occur in our area.

Mertensia longiflora
forma alba

INDEX

BIBLIOGRAPHY

CLARK, Lewis J. *Wild Flowers of British Columbia*, Sidney, B.C. Gray's Publishing, 1973.

HITCHCOCK, CRONQUIST, OWNBEY & THOMPSON *Vascular Plants of the Pacific Northwest*, (University of Washington Press, 1964).

LARRISON, PATRICK, BAKER & YAICH *Washington Wildflowers*, (Seattle Audubon Society, 1974).

NIEHAUS, T.F. and RIPPER, C.L. *A Field Guide to Pacific States Wildflowers*, Boston: Houghton Mifflin Co., 1973.